The big hole

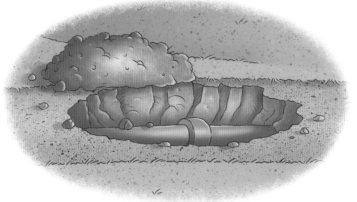

Rigby

A Harcourt Achieve Imprint

www.Rigby.com
1-800-531-5015

Look at the cars.

Look at the big hole!

Here is the digger.

Look at the digger.

8

Here is the big truck.

10

Look at the big truck.

12

Here is the roller.

Look at the roller.

Look at the cars.